Classic
CAJUN

Classic

CAJUN

Hot and spicy Louisiana cooking

FOREWORD BY
RUBY LE BOIS

This edition published in 1996 by
SMITHMARK Publishers, a division of US Media Holdings, Inc.
16 East 32nd Street
New York NY 10016
USA
SMITHMARK books are available for bulk purchase for sales promotion and for premium use.
For details write or call the manager of Special Sales, SMITHMARK Publishers Inc.
16 East 32nd Street, New York, NY 10016; (212) 532-6600

Produced by Anness Publishing Limited
1 Boundary Row
London SE1 8HP

ISBN 0-7651-9863-0

Publisher Joanna Lorenz
Senior Cookery Editor Linda Fraser
In-house Editor Anne Hildyard
Designer Nigel Partridge
Illustrations Madeleine David
Photographers Edward Allwright, Steve Baxter, James Duncan and Amanda Heywood
Recipes Carla Capalbo, Sarah Gates, Ruby Le Bois, Laura Washburn and Steven Wheeler
Food for photography Jane Hartshorn, Elizabeth Wolf-Cohen and Wendy Lee
Stylists Hilary Guy and Blake Minton
Jacket photography Thomas Odulate

Produced by Anness Publishing Limited

Printed and bound in Singapore

Pictures on frontispiece and pages 7, 8 and 9: Zefa Pictures Ltd.

CONTENTS

FOREWORD

Visit New Orleans at any time of the year – especially during Mardi Gras – and you will find yourself swept up in a swirl of excitement. This is not just the city that never sleeps; it is the city that never stands still. Jazz pours from open doorways, drifts from piano bars and seems to sizzle in the very air you breathe. And wherever there is music, there is food. Wonderful gutsy, glorious food. Rich in color, often fiery but always full of flavor, Cajun cooking is unique.

Green bell pepper, celery and onions are favorite flavorings (used in combination so often that they are known as "The Holy Trinity"), but it is in spicing that the Cajun cook excels. Cayenne, black and white pepper and paprika are all grist to the cook's mill, and every family has its own spice mix.

With the Mississippi Delta on the doorstep, it comes as no surprise that seafood is a specialty. Redfish, catfish, crabs, snapper and sea bass come from the coastal waters, with the bayous providing freshwater fish and crawfish. Louisiana is famous for its oysters, which are particularly plump, sweet and succulent in the spring, when the beds are swept by the Mississippi flood waters.

When the early settlers made this area their home, they found plenty of game for the cooking pots. Smothered Rabbit, with its spicy onion and celery sauce, remains a popular dish, and small game birds such as quail are now farmed, along with poussin, duck and chicken. Louisianans are fond of pork, which was introduced by the early American settlers.

Cajuns love sweet, succulent vegetables; particularly corn, sweet potatoes and parsnips. Tomatoes, introduced by the Spanish, are also widely used, as is the okra that was contributed by West African slaves brought in to work the vast cotton plantations.

Sweet treats include Pecan Pie and the famous Pecan Nut Divinity Cake, both of which feature in this exciting collection of recipes.

This is more than a cookbook: it's an invitation, requesting your presence at a feast of fabulous flavors. Cajun cooking is one of the world's most exciting cuisines – enjoy it!

RUBY LE BOIS

INTRODUCTION

Like its sophisticated cousin, Creole cooking, Cajun cooking is predominantly French, with liberal dashes of Spanish, African and Native American influences. But unlike Creole cooking, which originated in the fine kitchens of wealthy French cotton plantation owners and was honed in the restaurants they frequented, Cajun cooking came from peasant stock, from an intrepid and enterprising group of farmers and fishermen whose arrival in Louisiana was the result of adversity rather than adventure.

These were the Acadians, French men and women who settled in Acadia (later to become Nova Scotia) in 1620, only to find themselves ousted by the British in 1713. They fled south, many ending up in the "French triangle" of southwestern Louisiana, a place as hot and humid as Canada had been cold and bracing. The adaptable Acadians embraced their new home with enthusiasm, remodeling the recipes of their forefathers to include the local game and seafood. From Native Americans they learned to gather wild herbs and berries, and how to use a mixture of ground sassafras and thyme (*filé*) as a thickener. West African cooks, brought to Louisiana to work the cotton plantations, introduced them to mysterious new vegetables, such as okra, which they called *n'gombo*. The name persists today as *gumbo*, a soup/stew made from seafood, meat, poultry or vegetables.

In the latter half of the 18th century, New Orleans was ruled by Spain, and new ingredients and cooking styles came on the

scene. Acadians, now known as Cajuns, took this in their stride. They learned to love paella (a perfect dish for this part of the world, with its abundant rice and seafood), adapting it in their own inimitable fashion and giving it a new name, "Jambalaya", in recognition of the ham (*jambon*) which was almost always included.

While traditional French peasant dishes survived, Cajun cooks were scaling new heights. They had discovered peppers in all their rich and wondrous variety. Fresh chilies, sweet peppers, cayenne pepper, paprika, ground black and white pepper – all were investigated, then incorporated into a constantly evolving cuisine. They borrowed from Creole cooks, too, and the boundaries between the two culinary styles began to blur.

Today, while Cajun cooking continues to be more robust than its "citified" Creole counterpart, it, too, has its subtle side. Bisques, brochettes and featherlight beignets happily coexist

Two street scenes in New Orleans: the east Pontalba building in the French quarter (above) and early evening in bustling Bourbon Street (left).

with blackened fish and baked sweet potatoes. The roux, that famous French thickening and flavoring agent, is common to both cuisines. Oil, rather than the more conventional butter, is heated and stirred with flour in a black iron pan and the mixture allowed to darken, the depth of color varying according to the individual recipe. Roux is so fundamental to both Cajun and Creole cooking that many cooks make up the various mixtures in bulk.

In 1803 New Orleans became part of the United States as a result of the Louisiana Purchase. With its cosmopolitan history, the city and its environs continued to attract immigrants from all over the globe. Each brought their cooking pots and favorite recipes, and each enriched – and was enriched by – Cajun cooking.

This marvelous trade continues today. Cajun cooks love experimenting with new ideas and ingredients, and expect all who try their recipes to do the same. So – if you find it difficult to obtain any of the ingredients in this book, do as those early Acadians did – adopt and adapt!

HOT PARSNIP FRITTERS ON BABY SPINACH

Fritters are a firm favorite of Cajun cooks, with their love for deep frying. The technique brings out the luscious sweetness of parsnips, here set on a walnut-dressed salad of tender baby spinach leaves.

INGREDIENTS

2 large parsnips

1 cup flour

1 egg, separated

½ cup milk

4 ounces baby spinach leaves

2 tablespoons olive oil

1 tablespoon walnut oil

1 tablespoon sherry vinegar

oil for deep frying

1 tablespoon coarsely chopped walnuts

salt, ground black pepper and

cayenne pepper

SERVES 4

1 Peel the parsnips, bring to a boil in a large pan of salted water and simmer for 10–15 minutes until tender but not mushy. Drain, cool and cut diagonally into slices about 2 x ½- inch.

2 Put the flour in a bowl, make a well in the center and add the egg yolk. Mix in with a fork, gradually stirring in the surrounding flour. Begin adding the milk, while continuing to mix in the flour. Season with salt, and black and cayenne peppers, and then beat with a whisk until the batter is completely smooth.

3 Discard any baby spinach leaves that are discolored or damaged, then wash the rest and dry them carefully. Place the leaves in a bowl. Make the dressing: in a screw-top jar, mix the olive and walnut oils, sherry vinegar, and salt and black pepper to taste. Shake the jar vigorously.

4 When ready to serve, whisk the egg white until it peaks softly. Fold in a little of the batter, then fold the white into the batter. Heat the oil for deep frying.

5 Toss the salad in the dressing. Arrange the dressed greens on four salad plates and scatter with walnuts.

6 Dip the parsnip slices in the batter and fry a few at a time until puffy and golden. Drain on paper towels and keep warm. To serve, arrange the fritters on the salad.

CORN CAKES WITH BROILED TOMATOES

I f you are short of time, use drained canned sweetcorn in place of the fresh corn on the cob in these delightful and tasty fritters.

INGREDIENTS
1 large corn on the cob
⅔ cup flour
1 egg
a little milk
2 large, firm tomatoes
1 garlic clove
1 teaspoon dried oregano
2–3 tablespoon oil, plus extra for shallow frying
8 cupped iceberg lettuce leaves
salt and ground black pepper
shredded fresh basil leaves, to garnish

SERVES 4

1 Pull the husks and silk away from the corn, then hold the cob upright on a board and cut downwards with a heavy knife to strip off the kernels. Place in a pan of boiling water and cook for 3 minutes after the water has returned to a boil, then drain through a colander and rinse under cold running water to cool quickly.

2 Put the flour into a bowl, make a well in the center and add the egg. Mix with a fork, gradually stirring in the flour, adding a little milk to make a soft dropping consistency. Add the corn and season.

3 Preheat the broiler. Halve the tomatoes horizontally and make two or three criss-cross slashes across the cut side of each half. Crush the garlic and rub it, the oregano and some salt and pepper over the cut surface of each half, then trickle with oil and broil until lightly browned.

4 Meanwhile, heat some oil in a wide frying pan and drop a large spoonful of batter into the center. Cook one cake at a time, over low heat, turning as soon as the top is set. Drain on paper towels and keep warm while cooking the remaining corn cakes. The mixture should make at least eight corn cakes.

5 Put two lettuce leaves on each of four serving plates, place two corn cakes on top, garnish with basil and serve with a broiled tomato half.

CRAB BAYOU

D on't be tempted to use canned crabmeat in this dish – the result will be disappointing. Fresh crab-meat is now available in most supermarkets.

INGREDIENTS

1 pound fresh lump crabmeat
3 hard-boiled egg yolks
1 teaspoon Dijon mustard
6 tablespoons butter or margarine, at room temperature
¼ teaspoon cayenne pepper
3 tablespoons sherry
2 tablespoons chopped fresh parsley
½ cup whipping cream
½ cup thinly sliced scallions, including some of the green stems
½ cup dried bread crumbs
salt and ground black pepper

SERVES 6

1 Preheat the oven to 350°F. Pick over the crabmeat and remove any shell or cartilage, keeping the pieces of crab as big as possible.

2 In a bowl, crumble the egg yolks with a fork. Add the mustard, 4 tablespoons of the butter or margarine, and the cayenne, and mash together to form a paste.

3 Mash in the sherry and parsley. Mix in the cream and scallions. Stir in the crabmeat. Season with salt and pepper.

4 Divide the mixture equally among six greased scallop shells or other individual baking dishes. Sprinkle with the dried bread crumbs and dot with the remaining butter or margarine.

5 Bake for about 20 minutes until bubbling hot and golden brown.

13

CORN AND CRAB BISQUE

A Louisiana classic, and certainly luxurious enough for a dinner party, which makes it well worth the trouble to prepare.

INGREDIENTS

4 large corn on the cob
2 bay leaves
1 cooked crab weighing about 2¼ pounds
2 tablespoons butter
2 tablespoons flour
1¼ cups whipping cream
6 scallions, shredded
salt, ground black and white pepper, and cayenne pepper
hot French bread, to serve (optional)

SERVES 8

1 Pull away the husks and silk from the corn, hold the cob upright on a board and cut downwards with a heavy knife to strip off the kernels, then set aside.

2 Put the stripped cobs into a deep saucepan with 12 cups cold water, the bay leaves and 2 teaspoons salt. Bring to a boil and let simmer until tender.

3 Pull away the two flaps between the big claws of the crab, stand it on its "nose" where the flaps were, and bang down firmly with the heel of your hand on the rounded end. Separate the crab from its top shell, keeping the shell.

4 Push out the mouth and abdominal sac immediately below the mouth, and discard. Pull away the gills around the central chamber and discard. Scrape out all the semi-liquid brown meat and keep it.

5 Crack the claws and extract all the white meat. Pick out the white meat from the central body. Set aside. Put the spidery legs and all the other pieces of shell into the pan with the corn cobs. Simmer for 15 minutes, then strain into a clean pan and boil rapidly to reduce to 8 cups.

6 Meanwhile, melt the butter in a small pan, add the flour and stir constantly over low heat until the roux is the color of rich cream. Off the heat, stir in 1 cup of the stock. Return to the heat, stir until thickened, then stir into the pan of strained stock. Add the corn kernels, return to a boil and simmer for 5 minutes.

7 Add the crabmeat, cream and scallions and season with salt, black pepper and cayenne pepper. Return to a boil and simmer for 2 minutes. Serve immediately with hot French bread, if using.

"POPCORN" WITH BASIL MAYONNAISE

Crispy battered seafood is served with a rich, herb mayonnaise for dipping. This is an ideal dish for an informal supper party.

INGREDIENTS
2 pounds raw crayfish tails, peeled, or
small shrimp, peeled and deveined
2 eggs
1 cup dry white wine
½ cup fine cornmeal
½ cup flour
1 tablespoon snipped fresh chives
1 garlic clove, minced
½ teaspoon fresh thyme leaves
¼ teaspoon salt
¼ teaspoon cayenne pepper
¼ teaspoon ground black pepper
oil for deep frying

FOR THE MAYONNAISE
1 egg yolk
2 teaspoons Dijon mustard
1 tablespoon white wine vinegar
salt and ground black pepper
1 cup olive or vegetable oil
½ cup basil leaves, chopped

SERVES 8

1 Rinse the crayfish tails or shrimp in cold water. Drain well and set aside in a cool place until needed.

2 Using a fork, whisk together the eggs and dry white wine in a small bowl, then set aside in a cool place.

3 In a mixing bowl, combine the cornmeal, flour, chives, garlic, thyme, salt and pepper, and the cayenne pepper. Gradually whisk in the egg mixture, blending well. Cover the batter and then let stand for about 1 hour at room temperature.

4 For the mayonnaise, combine the egg yolk, mustard and vinegar in a mixing bowl. Add salt and pepper to taste. Add the oil in a thin stream, beating vigorously with a wire whisk. When the mixture is thick and smooth, stir in the basil. Cover and chill.

5 Heat 2–3 inches of oil in a large frying pan or deep-fryer to 375°F. Dip the seafood into the batter and fry in small batches for 2–3 minutes, turning to color evenly until golden brown. Remove with a slotted spoon and drain on paper towels. Serve hot with the basil mayonnaise.

CORN AND SHRIMP BISQUE

This creamy soup is quite filling, so provide a light main course to follow if serving as an appetizer at a lunch or dinner party.

INGREDIENTS
2 tablespoons olive oil
1 onion, chopped
4 tablespoons butter or margarine
¼ cup flour
3 cups fish or chicken stock, or clam juice
1 cup milk
1 cup peeled, cooked small shrimp,
deveined if necessary
1½ cups corn, fresh, frozen or canned
½ teaspoon chopped fresh dill or thyme
salt and hot pepper sauce
½ cup light cream
fresh dill sprigs and shrimp, to garnish

SERVES 4

1 Heat the olive oil in a large heavy-based saucepan. Add the onion and cook over a low heat for about 8–10 minutes until softened.

2 Meanwhile, melt the butter or margarine in a medium saucepan. Add the flour and stir with a wire whisk until blended. Cook for 1–2 minutes. Pour in the stock or clam juice, and milk and stir to blend. Bring to a boil over medium heat and cook for 5–8 minutes, stirring frequently.

3 Cut each shrimp in half and add to the onion with the corn and dill or thyme. Cook for 2–3 minutes, stirring occasionally. Remove the pan from the heat.

4 Add the sauce mixture to the shrimp and corn mixture and stir to mix well. Remove 3 cups of the soup and purée in a blender or food processor. Return it to the rest of the soup in the pan and stir well. Season with salt and hot pepper sauce to taste.

5 Add the cream and stir to blend. Heat the soup almost to boiling point, stirring frequently. Serve hot, garnished with sprigs of fresh dill, and shrimp.

GREEN HERB GUMBO

raditionally served at the end of Lent, this is a joyful, sweetly spiced and revitalizing dish.

INGREDIENTS

12-ounce piece raw smoked ham

2 tablespoons cooking oil

1 large Spanish onion, coarsely chopped

2–3 garlic cloves, crushed

1 teaspoon each dried oregano and thyme

2 bay leaves

2 cloves

2 celery stalks, finely sliced

1 green bell pepper, seeded and chopped

½ green cabbage, stalks removed and finely shredded

8 cups light stock

7 ounces collard greens or kale, finely shredded

7 ounces Chinese mustard cabbage, finely shredded (see Cook's Tip)

7 ounces spinach, shredded

1 bunch watercress, shredded

6 scallions, finely shredded

½ cup chopped fresh parsley

½ teaspoon ground allspice

1 teaspoon grated nutmeg

salt, ground black pepper and cayenne pepper

hot French bread or garlic bread, to serve

SERVES 6–8

1 Remove the fat and rind from the ham in one piece and set aside. Dice the ham quite finely. Put the fat piece with the oil into a deep saucepan and heat until it sizzles. Stir in the diced ham, onion, garlic, oregano and thyme, and stir over a moderate heat for about 5 minutes.

2 Add the bay leaves, cloves, celery and green bell pepper and stir for about another 2–3 minutes, then add the cabbage and stock. Bring to a boil and simmer for 5 minutes.

3 Add the collard greens or kale and Chinese mustard cabbage, boil for another 2 minutes, then add the spinach, watercress and scallions. Lower the heat and simmer for 1 minute after it returns to a boil, then add the parsley, ground allspice and nutmeg, salt, black pepper and cayenne to taste.

4 Remove the piece of ham fat and, if you can find them, the cloves. Serve the gumbo immediately with hot French bread or garlic bread.

COOK'S TIP

Chinese mustard cabbage is available in some supermarkets, as well as from oriental shops and markets. If, however, you can't find it, substitute turnip tops or kohlrabi leaves.

FROMAJARDIS

These cheese-filled pastry parcels are ideal to serve at a cocktail party. Try using a mixture of thyme, chives and sage in the filling.

INGREDIENTS
2 cups flour
¼ teaspoon grated nutmeg
½ teaspoon salt
10 tablespoons cold butter
6–8 tablespoons ice water

FOR THE FILLING
2 eggs
1 cup grated Cheddar cheese
hot pepper sauce
1 tablespoon chopped mixed fresh herbs

MAKES ABOUT 40

1 For the pastry, sift the flour, nutmeg and salt into a bowl. Using a pastry blender or two knives, cut the butter into the dry ingredients as quickly as possible until the mixture resembles coarse bread crumbs.

2 Sprinkle 6 tablespoons of the ice water over the flour mixture. Combine with a fork until the dough holds together. If the dough is too crumbly, add a little more water, 1 tablespoon at a time. Gather the dough into a ball.

3 Divide the dough in half and pat each portion into a ball. Wrap the balls in wax paper and chill for 20 minutes.

4 Preheat the oven to 425°F. For the filling, put the eggs in a bowl and beat well with a fork. Add the cheese, hot pepper sauce to taste, and the herbs.

5 On a lightly floured surface, roll out the dough to a thickness of ⅛- inch or less. Cut out rounds using a 3-inch pastry cutter or drinking glass.

6 Place 1 teaspoon of filling in the center of each pastry round. Fold over to make half-moon shapes, and press the edges together with the prongs of a fork. A little filling may ooze through the seams.

7 Cut a few small slashes in the top of each pastry with the point of a sharp knife. Place on ungreased cookie sheets. Bake for 18–20 minutes until the pastries start to darken slightly. To test, cut one in half; the pastry should be completely cooked through. Serve warm.

COOK'S TIP
The fromajardis may be made ahead of time. Let them cool on a wire rack and then store in an airtight container. Just before serving, reheat the pastries for 5–10 minutes in a preheated oven at 375°F.

FRIED FISH WITH TARTAR SAUCE
AND HUSH PUPPIES

T he story goes that fishermen would fry pieces of batter, then throw them to their dogs to hush them.

INGREDIENTS
1 cup cornmeal
½ cup flour
1½ teaspoons baking powder
1 garlic clove, crushed with
1 teaspoon salt
2 scallions, finely shredded
1 egg, lightly beaten
about 5 tablespoons milk
2 tablespoons butter

FOR THE FISH COATING
¼ cup flour
¼ cup cornstarch
½ cup cornmeal
½ teaspoon each dried oregano and thyme
1 teaspoon each salt, cayenne and
paprika
2 teaspoons dry mustard powder
1 egg
½ cup milk

FOR THE FISH FILLETS
oil for deep frying
4 plaice fillets, skinned
lemon slices and flat leaf parsley,
to garnish
tartar sauce, to serve

SERVES 4

1 To make the hush puppy batter, mix together the cornmeal, flour and baking powder and stir in the crushed garlic and scallions. Stir in the egg with a fork.

2 Heat 5 tablespoons of milk and the butter together slowly until the butter melts, then increase the heat and, when it boils, stir thoroughly into the dry ingredients, adding a little more milk if necessary to make a stiff dough. Allow to

3 To make the fish coating, mix the flour, cornstarch and cornmeal with the herbs and seasonings in a shallow dish. Beat the egg and milk together in another dish.

4 Scoop out pieces of hush puppy batter no bigger than a walnut and roll into balls between moistened hands. Heat the oil for deep-frying. Fry the hush puppies in batches, until golden brown. They will swell in cooking, and it's important that they are cooked right to the middle, so don't have the oil fiercely hot to start with. It should sizzle and froth up around them as you drop them in, but not brown them at once. Drain on paper towels and keep warm.

5 Coat the fish fillets, first in the egg mixture and then in the flour and cornmeal coating mixture. Fry the fillets two at a time for 2–3 minutes on each side, until crisp and golden brown, then drain on paper towels. Serve the fish fillets with the hush puppies and tartar sauce, garnished with lemon and parsley.

SPICED FISH

Cajun blackened fish is a specialty of Paul Prudhommes, a chef from New Orleans. Fillets of fish are coated with an aromatic blend of herbs and spices and pan-fried in butter.

INGREDIENTS

1 teaspoon dried thyme
1 teaspoon dried oregano
1 teaspoon ground black pepper
¼ teaspoon cayenne pepper
2 teaspoons paprika
½ teaspoon garlic salt
4 cod or red bream fillets, about
6 ounces each
6 tablespoons butter
½ red bell pepper, sliced
½ green bell pepper, sliced
fresh thyme, to garnish
broiled tomatoes and sweet potato purée,
to serve

SERVES 4

1 Place all the herbs, garlic salt and spices in a bowl and mix well. Dip the fish fillets in the spice mixture until lightly coated.

2 Heat 2 tablespoons of the butter in a large frying pan, add the peppers and fry for 4–5 minutes until softened. Remove the peppers and keep warm.

3 Add the remaining butter to the pan and heat until sizzling. Add the fish fillets and fry over moderate heat for 3–4 minutes on each side, until browned and cooked.

4 Transfer the fish fillets to a warmed serving dish, surround with the fried red and green pepper slices and garnish with fresh thyme. Serve the spiced fish with some broiled tomato halves and creamy sweet potato purée.

COOK'S TIP
This blend of herbs and spices can be used to flavor any fish steaks or fillets and could also be used to jazz up pan-fried shrimp.

FISH STEAKS WITH DILL-MUSTARD SAUCE

C atfish is the favorite choice of a firm white fish in Cajun cooking. Cod is a good alternative. Here, fish is fried to a light golden crust in butter and served with a pungent mustard sauce.

INGREDIENTS
FOR THE SAUCE
2 tablespoons Dijon mustard
⅔ cup mayonnaise
2 tablespoons finely chopped fresh dill

FOR THE FISH STEAKS
2 tablespoons milk
4 catfish or cod steaks, about
6 ounces each
2 tablespoons flour
2 teaspoons mustard powder
4 tablespoons butter
salt and ground black pepper
lemon wedges and fresh dill sprigs,
to garnish

SERVES 4

1 Mix all the ingredients for the sauce in a small bowl and put to one side until required.

2 Put the milk in a soup plate and lay the fish steaks in it. On a separate plate, mix the flour, mustard powder and seasoning.

3 Melt the butter in a frying pan. Turn the fish in the milk and dip immediately in the flour mixture, then shake off any excess.

4 When the butter sizzles, fry the fish steaks for 2–3 minutes on each side until the outside is crisp and pale golden and you can just pull the flesh from the bone with the sharp tip of a knife. Work in two batches if you need to, keeping the fish warm until ready to serve.

5 Serve as soon as possible, garnished with lemon wedges and sprigs of dill. Pass the sauce around separately.

CRAYFISH OR SHRIMP ETOUFFÉE

touffer means "to smother", and this seafood dish is certainly smothered in delectable flavors.

INGREDIENTS
2½ *pounds raw crayfish or shrimp in the shell, with heads left on*
3 cups water
⅓ *cup vegetable oil*
⅓ *cup flour*
¾ *cup chopped onions*
¼ *cup chopped green bell pepper*
¼ *cup chopped celery*
1 garlic clove, crushed
½ *cup dry white wine*
2 tablespoons butter or margarine
½ *cup chopped fresh parsley*
¼ *cup snipped fresh chives*
salt and hot pepper sauce
crayfish and flat leaf parsley, to garnish
rice, to serve

SERVES 6

1 Peel and devein the crayfish or shrimp; reserve the heads and shells. Place the seafood in a bowl, cover and chill.

2 Put the heads and shells in a large pan with the water. Bring to a boil, cover and simmer for 15 minutes. Strain and reserve 1½ cups of the stock.

3 To make the Cajun roux, heat the oil in a heavy cast-iron frying pan or steel saucepan. (Do not use a non-stick pan.)

4 When hot, gradually add the flour, and blend to a smooth paste using a long-handled flat-ended wooden spoon.

5 Cook over moderately low heat for about 25–40 minutes, stirring constantly, until the roux reaches the desired color. It will gradually deepen in color from light beige to tan, to a deeper, redder brown. When it reaches the color of peanut butter, remove the pan from the heat and immediately mix in the onions, bell pepper and celery. Stir to prevent further darkening.

6 Return the pan to low heat. Add the garlic and cook for 1–2 minutes, stirring constantly. Add the seafood stock and blend well with a wire whisk. Then whisk in the dry white wine.

7 Bring to a boil, stirring, and simmer for about 3–4 minutes until the sauce is thickened. Remove from the heat.

8 In a large heavy-based saucepan, melt the butter or margarine. Add the crayfish or shrimp, stir, and cook for about 2–3 minutes. Stir in the parsley and chives.

9 Add the sauce and stir well. Season with salt and hot pepper sauce to taste. Simmer for 3–4 minutes. Serve hot on a bed of rice, garnished with crayfish and parsley.

Trout with Pecan Nut Butter

This is the Cajun version of the classic French dish of trout with almonds and produces a subtly spiced and herby supper dish.

Ingredients

For the Pecan Nut Butter
½ cup shelled pecan nut halves, roasted
4 tablespoons sweet butter
2 teaspoons Worcestershire sauce
1 teaspoon lemon juice

For the Trout Fillets
4 large trout fillets, about 6 ounces each
2 teaspoons paprika
1 teaspoon cayenne pepper
1 teaspoon dried oregano
pinch of dried thyme
½ teaspoon garlic salt
1 teaspoon salt
1 egg
½ cup milk
3 tablespoons flour
oil for shallow frying
ground black pepper

Serves 4

1 Finely chop the pecan nuts in a blender or food processor. Add the butter, Worcestershire sauce and lemon juice, and blend well. Scrape out onto plastic wrap, roll into a sausage, wrap and chill.

2 Rinse the trout fillets under cold running water, then pat dry. Mix the paprika, cayenne, oregano, thyme and garlic salt with the salt and ground black pepper. Sprinkle a pinch on each fillet.

3 Beat the egg and milk in a shallow dish and add 1 teaspoon of the spice mix. In another dish, combine the remaining spice mix with the flour.

4 Heat the oil for shallow frying in a frying pan. Dip the trout fillets in the egg mixture, then in the seasoned flour, shaking off any excess. Fry, then drain on paper towels and keep warm. Serve the fillets with a slice of pecan butter on each.

OYSTER AND BACON BROCHETTES

S ix oysters per person makes a good appetizer, served with the seasoned oyster liquor to trickle over the skewers. Serve nine oysters per person with a cool salad as a main course.

INGREDIENTS
36 live oysters
18 thin-cut rashers bacon
1 cup flour
1 tablespoon paprika
1 teaspoon cayenne pepper
1 teaspoon salt
1 teaspoon garlic salt
2 teaspoons dried oregano
oil for shallow frying
ground black pepper
celery leaves and red chilies, to garnish

FOR THE SAUCE
½ red chili, seeded and very finely chopped
2 scallions, very finely chopped
2 tablespoons finely chopped fresh parsley
juice of ¼–½ lemon
salt and ground black pepper

SERVES 4–6

1 Shuck the oysters over a bowl. Wrap your hand in a dish towel and cup the deep shell of each oyster in it. Twist the point of a strong short-bladed knife into the hinge between the shells. Push the knife in and cut the muscle, holding the shell closed. Tip the liquor from the deep shell into the bowl. Cut the flesh free from the shell. Discard the shells.

2 For the sauce, mix the chili, scallions and parsley into the oyster liquor and sharpen with lemon juice. Season and transfer to a small bowl.

3 Halve the bacon rashers widthwise, wrap around each oyster, then thread onto four or six skewers. On a plate, mix the flour with the paprika, cayenne pepper, salt, garlic salt, oregano and black pepper. Roll the skewers in it, shaking off the excess.

4 Heat 1-inch of oil in a wide frying pan and fry the skewers in small batches for about 3–4 minutes over moderately hot heat, turning until crisp and brown. Drain on paper towels and serve garnished with the celery leaves and red chilies and accompanied by the sauce.

SHRIMP-STUFFED EGGPLANT

The rich, creamy texture of eggplant is beautifully set off by a herb and slightly spicy shrimp filling in this impressive-looking and great-tasting dish.

INGREDIENTS

2 large firm eggplants, of equal size
2 tablespoons lemon juice
3 tablespoons butter or margarine
8 ounces raw shrimp, peeled and deveined
½ cup thinly sliced scallions, including some green stems
4 tomatoes, chopped
1 garlic clove, crushed
¼ cup chopped fresh parsley
¼ cup chopped fresh basil 1T dried
pinch of grated nutmeg
hot pepper sauce
½ cup dried bread crumbs
salt and ground black pepper
rice, to serve

SERVES 4

1 Preheat the oven to 375°F. Cut the eggplants in half lengthwise. With a small sharp knife, cut around the inside edge of each eggplant half, about ½ inch from the skin. Carefully scoop out the flesh, leaving a shell ½- inch thick.

2 Immerse the eggplant shells, skin-side up, in cold water to prevent them from becoming discolored.

3 Chop the scooped-out eggplant flesh coarsely, toss with the lemon juice and set aside until needed.

4 Melt 2 tablespoons of the butter or margarine in a frying pan. Add the shrimp and sauté until pink, for about 2–3 minutes, turning so they cook evenly. Remove the shrimp with a slotted spoon and set aside.

5 Add the scallions to the frying pan and cook over medium heat for 2 minutes, stirring constantly. Add the tomatoes, garlic and parsley and cook for another 5 minutes.

+ dried basil
+ 2T white wine

6 Add the chopped eggplant, basil and nutmeg. If necessary, add a little water to prevent the vegetables from sticking. Mix well. Cover and simmer for 8–10 minutes, then remove from the heat.

7 Cut each shrimp into two. Stir into the vegetable mixture. Season with salt, black pepper and hot pepper sauce.

8 Lightly oil a shallow baking dish large enough to hold the eggplant halves in one layer. Drain and dry the eggplant shells and arrange in the dish.

9 Make a layer of bread crumbs in each shell. Add a layer of the shrimp mixture. Repeat, and finish with a layer of crumbs.

10 Dot with the remaining butter or margarine. Bake for about 20–25 minutes until bubbling hot and golden brown on top. Serve with rice.

FRIED FISH WITH PIQUANT SAUCE

Fried until golden brown, firm-textured fish fillets are accompanied by a cold, sharp-tasting sauce.

INGREDIENTS
1 egg
¼ cup olive oil
squeeze of lemon juice
½ teaspoon chopped fresh dill or parsley
4 catfish or cod fillets, about
6 ounces each
½ cup flour
2 tablespoons butter or margarine
salt and ground black pepper

FOR THE SAUCE
1 egg yolk
2 tablespoons Dijon mustard
2 tablespoons white wine vinegar
2 teaspoons paprika
½ cup olive or
vegetable oil
2 tablespoons creamed horseradish
½ teaspoon crushed garlic
¼ cup chopped celery
2 tablespoons tomato ketchup
½ teaspoon ground black pepper
½ teaspoon salt
mixed salad, to serve

SERVES 4

1 For the sauce, combine the egg yolk, mustard, vinegar and paprika in a mixing bowl. Add the oil in a thin stream, beating vigorously with a wire whisk to blend it in.

2 When the mixture is smooth and thick, beat in all the other sauce ingredients. Cover and chill until ready to serve.

3 Combine the egg, 1 tablespoon of the olive oil, the lemon juice, herbs and a little salt and pepper in a shallow dish. Beat until well combined.

4 Dip both sides of each fish fillet in the egg and herb mixture, then coat lightly with flour, shaking off the excess.

5 Heat the butter or margarine with the remaining olive oil in a large heavy-based frying pan. Add the fillets and fry for about 8–10 minutes until golden brown and cooked on both sides.

6 Transfer the fish to warmed serving plates and spoon some sauce on the top of each. Serve with a mixed salad.

SEAFOOD AND SAUSAGE GUMBO

This is a classic Cajun gumbo, with mussels, shrimp, crabmeat and chunks of wonderfully spicy sausage – a memorable dish.

INGREDIENTS
1 pound live mussels
1 pound shrimp
1 cooked crab weighing about 2¼ pounds
salt
1 small bunch parsley, leaves chopped and stalks reserved
⅔ cup oil
1 cup flour
1 green bell pepper, seeded and chopped
1 large onion, chopped
2 celery stalks, chopped
3 garlic cloves, finely chopped
3 ounces smoked spiced sausage, skinned and sliced
6 scallions, finely chopped
cayenne pepper
Tabasco sauce
salt
parsley, to garnish
cooked rice, to serve

SERVES 10–12

1 Wash the mussels in several changes of cold water, scrubbing away any barnacles and pulling off the black "beards" that protrude between the shells. Discard any broken mussels or any that are not closed.

2 Heat 1 cup of water in a pan. When it boils, add the mussels, cover tightly and cook for about 3 minutes over high heat, shaking often. As the mussels open, lift them out with tongs into a strainer set over a bowl. Discard any mussels that have not opened.

3 Shell the mussels, discarding the shells. Return the liquid from the bowl to the pan and add enough water to measure 9 cups.

4 Shell the shrimp and put the shells and heads into the pan. Remove the meat from the crab, separating the brown and white meat. Add the crab shell to the pan with 2 teaspoons salt. Bring to a boil, add the parsley stalks and simmer for 15 minutes. Cool, then strain. Add water to the liquid to measure 9 cups.

5 Make a roux with the oil and flour and stir until golden. Add the bell pepper, onion, celery and garlic. Cook for 3 minutes then add the sausage. Reheat the stock.

6 Add the brown crabmeat to the roux with the stock. Simmer for 30 minutes, then add the seafood, onions and seasoning. Serve with rice and garnish with parsley.

GLAZED DUCK BREASTS

Sweet potatoes accompany succulent sliced duck breast in this delicious dish. Choose a long, cylindrically shaped tuber.

INGREDIENTS

2 duck breast fillets, about 6 ounces each
1 pink-skinned sweet potato, about
14 ounces
2 tablespoons red currant jelly
1 teaspoon hot chili sauce
1 tablespoon sherry vinegar
4 tablespoons butter, melted
coarse sea salt and ground black pepper
green salad, to serve

SERVES 2

1 Slash the duck breast skin diagonally at 1-inch intervals and rub salt and pepper into the skin and cuts. Preheat the broiler with the shelf placed so that the meat will be 3–4 inches from the heat.

2 Scrub the sweet potato and cut into ½-inch thick slices, discarding the rounded ends.

3 Broil the meat, skin side up first, for 5 minutes, then flesh side up for 8–10 minutes, according to how pink you like your duck.

4 Meanwhile to make the glaze, warm the red currant jelly, hot chili sauce and sherry vinegar together in a heat proof bowl set in a pan of hot water, stirring to mix them as the jelly melts.

5 Remove the broiler pan from the heat, turn the duck breasts skin side up and paint with the glaze. Return to the broiler and cook for another 2–3 minutes until the glaze caramelizes. Transfer the duck breasts to a serving plate and keep warm.

6 Brush the sweet potato slices with melted butter and arrange in the broiler pan. Sprinkle with coarse sea salt and place one level higher under the broiler than the duck breasts were.

7 Cook the sweet potatoes for 4–5 minutes on each side until soft, brushing with more butter and sprinkling with sea salt and black pepper when you turn them.

8 Slice the glazed duck breast fillets and serve them with the broiled sweet potatoes and a fresh green salad on the side.

SMOTHERED RABBIT

Game has always formed a big part of the Cajun diet – it was the only meat available to the early settlers. The smothering technique gives plenty of flavor to a domestic rabbit.

INGREDIENTS
2 teaspoons salt
½ teaspoon garlic salt
½ teaspoon dried oregano
good pinch each of ground black pepper
and cayenne pepper
1 rabbit, skinned, cleaned and cut into
8 pieces
½ cup flour
4 tablespoons oil
1 onion, chopped
1 celery stalk, chopped
1 large garlic clove, crushed
1 bay leaf
1½ cups chicken stock
3 scallions, shredded
2 tablespoons chopped fresh parsley
snow peas and crusty bread, to serve

SERVES 4

1 Mix the salt, garlic salt, oregano, black pepper and cayenne together. Sprinkle the rabbit pieces lightly, using about half the seasoning mix, and pat it in thoroughly with your fingers.

2 Put the rest of the seasoning mix with the flour into a plastic bag, shake to mix, then shake the pieces of rabbit in this to dredge them, shaking off and reserving the excess until needed.

3 Heat the oil in a heavy flameproof casserole and fry the rabbit pieces, in batches, until browned on all sides. Set aside on a plate.

4 When all the rabbit is browned, cook the chopped onion and celery in the same pan for 5 minutes, stirring often. Add the garlic and bay leaf.

5 Heat the stock. Add 1 tablespoon of the seasoned flour to the oil in the pan and stir over the heat for 1 minute. Off the heat, gradually stir in some of the stock. When the sauce loosens, return to the heat and add the remaining stock, stirring constantly until boiling point is reached.

6 Lower the heat, return the rabbit pieces to the casserole, cover and simmer for about 1 hour, until the rabbit is very tender.

7 Check the seasoning and stir in the scallions and parsley. Serve with the snow peas and crusty bread.

CHICKEN SAUCE PIQUANTE

S auce Piquante goes with everything that runs, flies or swims in Louisiana – you will even find Alligator Sauce Piquante on menus. It is based on the brown Cajun roux and has red chilies to give it heat. Vary the heat by the number you use.

INGREDIENTS

4 chicken legs or 2 legs and 2 breasts
5 tablespoons oil
½ cup flour
1 onion, chopped
2 celery stalks, sliced
1 green bell pepper, seeded and diced
2 garlic cloves, crushed
1 bay leaf
½ teaspoon dried thyme
½ teaspoon dried oregano
1–2 red chilies, seeded and finely chopped
14-ounce can tomatoes, chopped, with their juice
1¼ cups chicken stock
salt and ground black pepper
watercress, to garnish
boiled potatoes, to serve

SERVES 4

1 Halve the chicken legs through the joint, or the breasts across the middle, to give eight pieces.

2 In a heavy frying pan, fry the chicken pieces in the oil until brown on all sides, lifting them out and setting them aside as they are done.

3 Strain the oil from the pan into a heavy flameproof casserole. Heat it and stir in the flour. Stir constantly over low heat until the roux is the color of peanut butter.

4 When the roux reaches the right stage, add the onion, celery and bell pepper and cook, stirring, for 2–3 minutes.

5 Add the garlic, bay leaf, thyme, oregano and chili(es). Stir for 1 minute, then add the tomatoes with their juice.

6 Gradually stir in the stock. Add the chicken pieces, cover and allow to simmer for 45 minutes, until the chicken is tender. If there is too much sauce or it is too runny, remove the lid for the last 10–15 minutes of the cooking time and increase the heat a little to concentrate the sauce.

7 Check the seasoning and serve garnished with watercress and accompanied by boiled potatoes.

POUSSINS WITH DIRTY RICE

This rice is called dirty not because of the bits in it but because jazz is called "dirty music", and the rice here is certainly jazzed up.

INGREDIENTS
FOR THE RICE
4 tablespoons cooking oil
¼ cup flour
4 tablespoons butter
1 large onion, chopped
2 celery stalks, chopped
1 green bell pepper, seeded and diced
2 garlic cloves, crushed
7 ounces minced pork
8 ounces chicken livers, sliced
Tabasco sauce
1¼ cups chicken stock
4 scallions, shredded
3 tablespoons chopped fresh parsley
generous 1 cup long-grain rice, cooked
salt and ground black pepper

FOR THE POUSSINS
4 poussins
2 bay leaves, halved
2 tablespoons butter
1 lemon
salt and ground black pepper

SERVES 4

1 In a small heavy saucepan, make a roux with 2 tablespoons of the oil and the flour. When it is a chestnut-brown color, remove the pan from the heat and place it immediately on a cold surface.

2 Heat the remaining oil with the butter in a frying pan and stir-fry the onion, celery and bell pepper for about 5 minutes.

3 Add the garlic and pork and stir-fry for 5 minutes, breaking up the pork and stirring to cook it all over.

4 Add the livers and fry for 2–3 minutes until they have changed color. Season with salt, pepper and Tabasco sauce.

5 Stir the roux into the pan and gradually add the stock. When it bubbles, cover and cook for about 30 minutes, stirring occasionally. Uncover the pan and cook for another 15 minutes, stirring frequently.

6 Preheat the oven to 400°F. Mix the scallions and parsley into the meat mixture and stir it all into the cooked rice, mixing well.

7 Put ½ bay leaf and 1 tablespoon of rice into each poussin. Rub the outside with the butter and season with salt and pepper.

8 Put the birds on a rack in a roasting pan, squeeze the juice from the lemon over them and roast for 35–40 minutes, basting twice with the pan juices.

9 Put the remaining rice into a shallow ovenproof dish, cover, and place on a low shelf in the oven for about the last 15–20 minutes of the birds' cooking time.

10 Serve the birds on a bed of dirty rice with the roasting pan juices (drained of fat) poured over.

BLACKENED CHICKEN BREASTS

The chicken breast pieces are fried quite quickly in this dish, causing the outside to become black and crispy while the inside remains soft and deliciously juicy.

INGREDIENTS
6 skinless, boneless chicken breast halves
6 tablespoons butter or margarine
1 teaspoon garlic powder
2 teaspoons onion powder
1 teaspoon cayenne pepper
2 teaspoons paprika
1½ teaspoons salt
½ teaspoon white pepper
1 teaspoon black pepper
¼ teaspoon ground cumin
1 teaspoon dried thyme
salad, to serve

SERVES 6

1 Slice each chicken breast piece in half horizontally, making two pieces of about the same thickness. Flatten slightly with the heel of your hand.

2 Melt the butter or margarine in a small saucepan, being very careful that it does not burn.

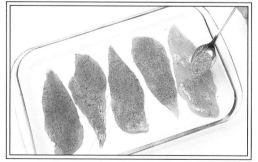

3 Combine all the remaining ingredients in a bowl. Brush the chicken pieces on both sides with melted butter or margarine, then sprinkle with the seasoning mixture.

4 Heat a large heavy frying pan over high heat, with no fat in it, until a drop of water sprinkled on the surface sizzles. This will take 5–8 minutes.

5 Drizzle a teaspoon of melted butter on each chicken piece. Place them in the frying pan in an even layer, two or three at a time. Cook for about 2–3 minutes until the underside begins to blacken. Turn and cook the other side for another 2–3 minutes. Keep the cooked pieces hot while cooking the remaining pieces. Serve hot with salad.

CHICKEN JAMBALAYA

T he secret of a good jambalaya is to make sure that the rice grains are well coated in oil before adding the liquid. This way they won't stick together while cooking.

INGREDIENTS
2½ pounds fresh chicken
1½ onions
1 bay leaf
1 parsley sprig
4 black peppercorns
2 tablespoons vegetable oil
2 garlic cloves, chopped
1 green bell pepper, seeded and chopped
1 celery stalk, chopped
generous 1 cup long-grain rice
4 ounces chorizo sausage, sliced
⅔ cup chopped, cooked ham
14-ounce can chopped tomatoes
with herbs
½ teaspoon hot chili powder
½ teaspoon cumin seeds
½ teaspoon ground cumin
1 teaspoon dried thyme
1 cup cooked, peeled shrimp
dash of Tabasco sauce
chopped parsley, to garnish

SERVES 4

1 Place the chicken in a large flameproof casserole and pour in 2½ cups of water. Add ½ onion, bay leaf, parsley and peppercorns and bring to a boil. Cover and simmer for about 1½ hours.

2 When the chicken is cooked, lift it out of the stock, skin, bone and chop the meat. Strain the stock, cool and reserve.

3 Chop the remaining onion and heat the oil in a large frying pan. Add the onion, garlic, green bell pepper and celery. Fry for about 5 minutes, then stir in the rice. Add the sausage, ham and chopped chicken and fry for another 2–3 minutes, stirring the mixture frequently.

4 Add the tomatoes and 1¼ cups of the stock and add the chili, cumin and thyme. Bring to a boil, cover and simmer for 20 minutes, or until the rice is tender and the liquid is absorbed.

5 Stir in the shrimp and Tabasco. Cook for 5 minutes, then season and serve.

LOUISIANA RICE

Some of the minced pork becomes slightly crispy in this rice dish, providing a variety of textures in a one-pan meal.

INGREDIENTS

4 tablespoons vegetable oil
1 small eggplant, diced
8 ounces chopped pork
4-ounce chicken thigh, chopped
1 red bell pepper, seeded and chopped
2 stalks celery, chopped
1 onion, chopped
1 garlic clove, crushed
1 teaspoon cayenne pepper
1 teaspoon paprika
1 teaspoon black pepper
½ teaspoon salt
1 teaspoon dried thyme
½ teaspoon dried oregano
2 cups chicken stock
8 ounces chicken livers, chopped
scant ¾ cup long-grain rice
1 bay leaf
3 tablespoons chopped fresh parsley
celery leaves, to garnish

SERVES 4

1 Heat the oil in a frying pan until very hot, then add the eggplant and stir-fry for about 5 minutes.

2 Add the pork and cook for 6–8 minutes, until browned. Add the chicken, mix well, cover, and cook for 10 minutes.

3 Add the bell pepper, celery, onion, garlic and all the spices and herbs. Cover and cook over high heat for 5–6 minutes, stirring frequently from the base of the pan.

4 Stir in the stock, cover and cook for 6 minutes. Add the livers; cook for about 2 minutes. Add the rice and bay leaf.

5 Cover and simmer for 6 minutes. Turn off the heat and let sit for about another 15 minutes. Remove the bay leaf and stir in the parsley. Serve hot.

PORK CHOPS WITH LEMON AND GARLIC SAUCE

This great recipe comes from the McIlhenny family, producers of Tabasco sauce. They like their food hot. Cautious cooks can start off with less Tabasco, adding more at the end of cooking.

INGREDIENTS
4 pork chops, about 6 ounces each
½ cup butter
½ lemon
1 tablespoon Worcestershire sauce
1½ teaspoons Tabasco sauce
1 garlic clove, finely chopped
salt and ground black pepper
broiled peppers and tomatoes, to serve

SERVES 4

1 Preheat the broiler. Arrange the chops in the broiler pan but do not place them under the broiler.

2 Melt the butter in a small non-aluminum saucepan. Squeeze in the juice of the lemon and bring to simmering point.

3 Add the sauces, and without browning the garlic, continue cooking over low heat for 5 minutes. Season.

4 Brush the tops of the chops liberally with the sauce, place the pan under the broiler and cook for about 5 minutes until they begin to brown.

5 Turn the chops and brush with more sauce. Broil for another 5 minutes or so, depending on the thickness of the chops. You can trickle a little more of the sauce on to serve. Serve the chops with broiled peppers and tomatoes.

ROAST PORK WITH CAJUN STUFFING

The familiar trinity of onion, celery and green bell pepper gives a Cajun flavor to this handsome roast – complete with crackling.

INGREDIENTS
3–3½ pounds boned loin of pork
1 tablespoon salt
1 teaspoon each ground black pepper,
cayenne pepper, paprika and
dried oregano
2 tablespoons cooking oil or
2 tablespoons lard
1 small onion, finely chopped
1 celery stalk, finely chopped
½ green bell pepper, seeded and
finely chopped
1 garlic clove, crushed

SERVES 6

1 If the pork is already tied up, untie it. Score the pork skin closely to make good crackling (you can ask your butcher to do this). Rub 2 teaspoons of the salt into the skin the night before if you can or, if not, as far ahead of cooking as possible on the day. If the meat has been chilled overnight, stand it in an airy place at room temperature for at least 2 hours before cooking.

2 Preheat the oven to 425°F. Mix the black pepper, cayenne, paprika and oregano with the remaining salt and rub over the fleshy side of the meat.

3 Heat the oil or lard and gently fry the onion, celery and green bell pepper for about 5 minutes, adding the garlic for the last minute of cooking time.

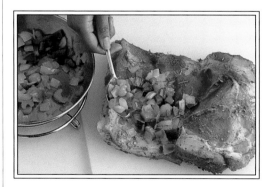

4 Spread the softened vegetable mixture evenly over the inside of the meat, right up to the edges.

5 Carefully roll up the loin of pork, skin side out, and tie in several places so that it holds its shape while cooking.

6 Roast the meat on a rack in a roasting pan. After 30 minutes, reduce the oven temperature to 350°F. Baste with the pan juices after 15 minutes and again every 20 minutes.

7 The overall roasting time will be about 2 hours. If the crackling does not go crisp and bubbly in the latter stages, increase the oven temperature a little for the last 20–30 minutes.

8 Allow the meat to rest in a warm place for 10–15 minutes before carving. This sets the juices.

MAQUE CHOUX

A Cajun classic, good with ham and chicken. Some cooks add a little sugar to heighten the sweetness, but for most, the natural sweetness of the corn is enough.

INGREDIENTS
4 tablespoons butter
1 large onion, finely chopped
1 green bell pepper, seeded and diced
2 large tomatoes, skinned and chopped
4 cups frozen corn
kernels, thawed
½ cup milk
salt, ground black pepper and
cayenne pepper

SERVES 4–6

1 Melt half the butter in a large pan and soften the onion in it, stirring regularly over a low heat for about 10 minutes until it begins to turn pale gold. Add the green bell pepper and stir over the heat for another minute, then add the tomatoes and let cook gently while preparing the corn.

2 Put the corn kernels and milk into a blender or food processor and process in brief bursts to break up the kernels to a porridge consistency.

3 Stir the corn mixture thoroughly into the pan and cook, partly covered, over a low heat for 20 minutes. Stir regularly, making sure that it does not stick to the base of the pan. If the mixture becomes too dry, add a little more milk. If it is rather wet in the latter stages, uncover, increase the heat a little and stir constantly for the last 5 minutes to thicken it.

4 Stir in the rest of the butter and season generously with salt, black pepper and cayenne. Serve hot.

BAKED SWEET POTATOES

S weet potatoes go well with all of the favorite Cajun seasonings: plenty of salt, white pepper as well as black and cayenne pepper, and lavish quantities of butter. Serve each person with half a potato as an accompaniment to meat, sausages or fish, or a whole one as a supper dish, perhaps topped with crispy bacon.

INGREDIENTS
3 sweet potatoes, about 1 pound each
6 tablespoons butter, sliced
salt and black pepper, white pepper and
cayenne pepper
flat leaf parsley, to garnish

SERVES 3–6

1 Wash the potatoes, leaving them wet. Rub salt into the skins and prick them all over. Place on the middle oven shelf. Turn on the oven at 400°F and bake for 1 hour, until the flesh feels soft.

2 The potatoes can either be served in halves or whole. For halves, split each one lengthwise and make close diagonal cuts in the flesh of each half. Then spread with slices of butter, and work the butter and seasonings roughly into the cuts.

3 Alternatively, if the potatoes are to be served whole, cut along the length of each potato. Open them slightly and put in butter slices along the length, seasoning with salt and black pepper, white pepper and cayenne pepper. Garnish with parsley.

ROASTED POTATOES, PEPPERS AND SHALLOTS

Based on a dish which is served at the Commander's Palace, this is in the new, rather more elegant style of New Orleans restaurant cooking.

INGREDIENTS
1¼ pounds waxy potatoes
12 shallots
2 yellow bell peppers
corn oil or olive oil
2 sprigs fresh rosemary
salt and ground black pepper

SERVES 4

COOK'S TIP
Although lamb does not feature prominently in Cajun cooking, this would certainly be a fine all-in-one vegetable dish to accompany it. It would also be good with roast chicken.

1 Preheat the oven to 400°F. Wash the potatoes and then blanch for 5 minutes in boiling water. Drain and, when they are cool enough to handle, skin and halve them lengthwise.

2 Peel the shallots, allowing them to fall into their natural segments. Cut each yellow bell pepper lengthwise into eight strips, discarding the seeds and pith.

3 Oil a shallow ovenproof dish thoroughly with corn oil or olive oil (corn oil is more authentic, olive oil tastes better). Assemble the potatoes and peppers in alternating rows and stud with the shallots.

4 Cut the rosemary sprigs into 2-inch lengths and tuck among the vegetables. Season the dish generously with corn oil or olive oil, salt and pepper, and bake in the oven, uncovered, for 30–40 minutes until all the vegetables are tender.

SPOONBREAD

This tasty cornmeal bread is so delightfully light that it has to be served with a spoon. Make sure you provide generous quantities of good quality butter to go with it.

INGREDIENTS
2½ cups milk
1 cup yellow cornmeal
6 tablespoons butter or margarine
1 teaspoon salt
1½ teaspoons baking powder
3 eggs, separated

SERVES 4

1 Preheat the oven to 375°F. Heat the milk in a heavy-based saucepan. Just before it boils, beat in the cornmeal with a wire whisk. Cook over low heat for about 10 minutes, stirring constantly.

2 Remove the pan from the heat and then beat in the butter or margarine, the salt and baking powder, whisking well until the mixture is completely smooth and the butter or margarine has melted.

3 Add the egg yolks, one at a time, and beat until the spoonbread batter is smooth and creamy.

4 In a large bowl, beat the egg whites until they form stiff peaks. Fold them into the cornmeal mixture.

5 Pour the batter into a well-greased 6¼-cup baking dish. Bake for 30–40 minutes until the bread is puffed and brown. Use a spoon to serve the bread. Hand around butter separately.

SPICED EGGPLANT FRIED IN CORNMEAL

These crisp eggplant slices are very good with plain broiled meat, poultry or fish. They can be served instead of meat in a vegetarian meal.

INGREDIENTS
1 large eggplant
salt
1 egg
½ cup milk
½ teaspoon paprika
½ teaspoon cayenne pepper
½ teaspoon ground black pepper
½ teaspoon garlic salt
scant 1 cup fine cornmeal
oil for deep frying

SERVES 3–4

1 Cut the eggplant into ½-inch thick slices. Sprinkle lightly with salt and stack them in a colander. Let stand in the sink to drain for 30 minutes, then wipe the slices dry on paper towels.

2 Beat the egg lightly in a shallow bowl with the milk, spices, pepper and garlic salt. Spread the cornmeal on a plate. Heat the oil for deep frying.

3 Dip each slice of eggplant in the spiced egg mixture, allowing the excess to drip back into the bowl. Turn the slice in the cornmeal, and drop immediately into the oil.

4 Fry three or four slices at a time, turning once, until they are golden on both sides. Drain on paper towels and keep warm until all the slices are fried. Serve hot.

BLACK-EYED PEA SALAD

This hearty, simple-to-make salad is served warm so that the flavors absorbed by the peas may be enjoyed at their fullest.

INGREDIENTS
2 small red peppers
½ teaspoon Dijon mustard
2 tablespoons wine vinegar
¼ teaspoon salt
pinch of ground black pepper
6 tablespoons olive oil
2 tablespoons snipped fresh chives
15-ounce can black-eyed peas
1 bay leaf
8 lean bacon rashers
flat leaf parsley, to garnish

SERVES 4

1 Preheat the broiler. When hot, broil the peppers until the skins blacken and blister, turning them so that all sides are charred. Remove from the broiler and seal in a paper bag. Let sit for 10 minutes.

2 Peel off the skins. Cut the peppers in half, discard the seeds, white pith and stem, and slice into ½ x 2-inch strips. Set aside.

3 Combine the mustard and vinegar in a small bowl. Add the salt and pepper. Beat in the oil until well blended. Add the minced fresh chives.

4 Drain and rinse the black-eyed peas. Heat the peas with the bay leaf for about 5 minutes, until just warmed through.

5 Meanwhile, cook the bacon until crisp. Drain on paper towels, then cut or break into small pieces.

6 Drain the peas and discard the bay leaf. While still warm, toss the beans with the chive dressing.

7 Make a mound of peas on a serving dish. Sprinkle with the bacon and serve, garnished with red pepper and parsley.

COOK'S TIP
If preferred, chop the peppers and mix into the warm peas at step 6.

POOR BOY STEAK SALAD

P oor Boy started life in the Italian Creole community of New Orleans when the poor survived on sandwiches filled with leftover scraps. Times have improved since then, and today the sandwich is commonly filled with tender beefsteak and other goodies. This is a salad version of "Poor Boy."

INGREDIENTS

4 sirloin steaks, about 6 ounces each
1 escarole lettuce
1 bunch watercress
4 tomatoes, quartered
4 large pickles, sliced
4 scallions, sliced
4 canned artichoke hearts, halved
6 ounces button mushrooms, sliced
12 green olives
½ cup Italian dressing
salt and ground black pepper

SERVES 4

1 Season the steaks with black pepper. Cook the steaks under a moderate broiler for 6–8 minutes, turning once, until medium-rare. Cover and let rest in a warm place until needed.

2 Wash and dry the greens. Combine with the rest of the ingredients (except the steaks) and toss in the Italian dressing.

3 Divide the salad among four plates. Slice each steak diagonally and position over the salad. Season with salt and serve.

PECAN PIE

This is a favorite pie all over the southern states, where pecan nuts flourish. It is delicious served warm with cream or ice cream.

INGREDIENTS
FOR THE PASTRY
1¾ cups flour
pinch of salt
½ cup butter
ice water
dried beans or rice, for baking blind

FOR THE FILLING
3 eggs
good pinch of salt
1 teaspoon vanilla extract
scant 1 cup well-packed brown sugar
4 tablespoons light corn syrup
4 tablespoons butter, melted
1 cup chopped pecan nuts, plus 12 pecan nut halves
whipped cream or vanilla ice cream, to serve

SERVES 6

1 For the pastry, mix the flour with the salt, then rub in the butter with your fingertips to a coarse sand consistency. Add ice water a little at a time, mixing first with a fork, then with your hand, until the mixture gathers into a dough.

2 Wrap the dough in plastic wrap and chill for 30–40 minutes. Preheat the oven to 375°F for 20 minutes.

3 Grease an 8–9-inch loose-based springform pan. Roll out the pastry to line the pan, pressing it into place with your fingers.

4 Run the rolling pin over the top of the pan to trim the extra pastry, giving a neat finish to the pastry shell.

5 Prick the pastry base with a fork and line with foil. Fill with dried beans or rice and bake blind for 15 minutes, then remove the foil and beans or rice and bake for another 5 minutes. Take the pastry shell from the oven and lower the oven temperature to 350°F.

6 Meanwhile, to make the filling, beat the eggs lightly with the salt and vanilla extract, then beat in the sugar, syrup and melted butter. Finally, mix in the chopped pecan nuts.

7 Spread the mixture in the half-baked pastry shell and bake for 15 minutes, then take it from the oven and stud with the pecan nut halves in a circle.

8 Return to the oven and bake for another 20–25 minutes until a thin metal skewer inserted gently into the center comes out clean.

9 Cool the pie for 10–15 minutes and serve it warm with whipped cream or a scoop of vanilla ice cream. Any leftover pie may be served cold.

PRALINES

Pronounced with a long "a" and the stress on the first syllable, these resemble puddles of nut fudge more than the crisp cookies Europeans think of as pralines. In Louisiana they are eaten as a dessert or whenever it seems a good idea to have something sweet with a cup of coffee.

INGREDIENTS
2 cups pecan nut halves
2 cups well-packed light brown sugar
1 cup granulated sugar
1¼ cups heavy cream
¾ cup milk
1 teaspoon vanilla extract

MAKES ABOUT 30 PIECES

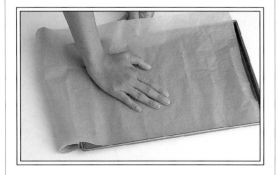

1 Roughly chop half of the pecan nuts and set all the nuts aside. Line 2–3 baking sheets with baking parchment.

2 Mix together the brown sugar, granulated sugar, cream and milk in a saucepan over moderate heat. Stir continuously until the mixture reaches 238°F on a sugar thermometer.

3 Remove from the heat immediately and beat with an electric beater or a balloon whisk until the mixture loses its sheen and becomes creamy in texture and grainy looking. This could take 15 minutes by hand or about 5 minutes with an electric beater.

4 Stir in the vanilla and nuts and drop large spoonfuls of the mixture onto the baking sheets. Leave to cool and set.

BANANAS FOSTER

A now-famous dessert named after Dick Foster, who was on the Vice Committee and therefore in charge of cleaning up the French Quarter of New Orleans in the 1950s.

INGREDIENTS

¾ cup light brown sugar

½ teaspoon ground cinnamon

½ teaspoon grated nutmeg

4 tablespoons butter

4 tablespoons banana liqueur

5 tablespoons dark rum

4 firm bananas, peeled and halved lengthwise

4 scoops firmly frozen vanilla ice cream, to serve

SERVES 4

1 Mix the sugar, cinnamon and nutmeg in a bowl. Melt the butter in a frying pan and add the sugar and spice mixture.

2 Add the liqueur and rum and stir over the heat until the sauce is syrupy.

3 Add the bananas and heat through, turning with a spoon to coat with the sauce.

4 If you are cooking over gas, tilt the pan to set alight the sauce. If your stove is electric, light the sauce with a match. Hold the pan at arm's length while you do this.

5 As soon as the flames die down, put pieces of banana on each plate with a scoop of ice cream. Pour on the sauce and serve immediately.

COOK'S TIP
You can vary the flavor with praline or walnut ice cream.

MISSISSIPPI MUD CAKE

I f you do not have a bundt pan, an ordinary ring mold will do – it will not alter the glorious taste of this rich dessert!

INGREDIENTS
2 cups flour
pinch of salt
1 teaspoon baking powder
*1¼ cups strong
brewed coffee*
¼ cup bourbon or brandy
5 ounces semisweet chocolate
1 cup butter or margarine
2 cups sugar
2 eggs, at room temperature
1½ teaspoons vanilla extract
cocoa powder for dusting
*sweetened whipped cream or ice cream,
to serve*

SERVES 8–10

1 Preheat the oven to 275°F. Sift the flour, salt and baking powder together into a mixing bowl and set aside until required.

2 Combine the coffee, bourbon or brandy, chocolate and butter or margarine in the top of a double boiler or in a bowl set over a pan of simmering water. Heat until the chocolate and butter have melted and the mixture is smooth, stirring occasionally.

3 Pour the chocolate mixture into a large bowl. Using an electric mixer on low speed, gradually beat in the sugar. Continue beating until the sugar has dissolved.

4 Increase the speed to medium and add the sifted dry ingredients. Mix well, then beat in the eggs and vanilla until thoroughly blended and smooth.

5 Pour the mixture into a well-greased 12½-cup bundt pan that has been dusted lightly with cocoa powder. Bake for 1 hour 20 minutes in the oven until a skewer inserted in the cake comes out completely clean.

6 Allow the cake to cool in the bundt pan for about 15 minutes, then unmold it onto a wire rack and set aside until it is completely cooled.

7 When the cake is cold, dust it lightly with cocoa powder. Serve with sweetened whipped cream or ice cream, if desired. Use vanilla, or other flavors of ice cream if you prefer.

CORNMEAL SCONES

For a morning snack or a tea time treat there is nothing better than scones, hot from the oven and spread with plenty of butter.

INGREDIENTS

1¼ cups flour

2½ teaspoons baking powder

¾ teaspoon salt

*½ cup cornmeal, plus more
for sprinkling*

*5 tablespoons white vegetable fat or
cold butter*

¾ cup milk

butter or margarine, to serve

MAKES ABOUT 12

1 Preheat the oven to 450°F. Sift the dry ingredients. Stir in the cornmeal. Rub in the fat or butter until the mixture resembles coarse meal.

2 Make a well in the center and pour in the milk. Stir in quickly with a wooden spoon for 1 minute, until the dough begins to pull away from the sides of the bowl.

3 Turn the dough onto a lightly floured surface and knead lightly 8–10 times only. Roll out to a thickness of ½ inch. Cut into rounds with a floured 2-inch cookie cutter. Do not twist the cutter.

4 Sprinkle an ungreased cookie sheet lightly with cornmeal. Arrange the scones on the sheet, about 1-inch apart. Sprinkle the scones with more cornmeal.

5 Bake until golden brown, for about 10–12 minutes. Serve the scones hot, with butter or margarine.

FRENCH QUARTER BEIGNETS

These lightly spiced, deep fried fritters are so easy to make and welcome at any time of day, with a sprinkling of confectioner's sugar.

INGREDIENTS
2 cups flour
1 teaspoon salt
1 tablespoon baking powder
1 teaspoon ground cinnamon
2 eggs
¼ cup sugar
¾ cup milk
½ teaspoon vanilla extract
oil for deep frying
confectioner's sugar, for sprinkling

MAKES ABOUT 20

1 To make the dough, sift the flour, salt, baking powder and ground cinnamon into a large mixing bowl. Cover and set aside until required.

2 In a separate bowl, beat together the eggs, sugar, milk and vanilla extract. Mix this into the flour mixture to form a dough.

3 Turn the dough onto a lightly floured surface and knead until smooth and elastic. Roll it out to a circle ¼-inch thick. Slice diagonally into diamonds about 3 inches long.

4 Heat oil in a deep-fryer or large, heavy-based saucepan to 375°F. Fry the beignets in the oil, a few at a time, turning once, until golden brown. Remove with a slotted spoon and drain well on kitchen paper towels. Before serving, sprinkle the beignets with confectioner's sugar.

PECAN NUT DIVINITY CAKE

T his three-layered cake, with its meringue-style icing, tastes truly heavenly. It looks impressive but is surprisingly simple to make.

INGREDIENTS
2½ cups pecan nuts
3 cups flour
1½ teaspoons baking powder
½ teaspoon salt
1 cup sweet butter, at
room temperature
2 cups sugar
5 eggs
1 cup milk
1 teaspoon vanilla extract

FOR THE DIVINITY ICING
3 cups confectioner's sugar
3 egg whites, at room temperature
2 drops vanilla essence

SERVES 6–8

1 Toast the pecan nuts in batches in a heavy-based pan over high heat, tossing regularly until they darken and give off a toasted aroma. Cool, then chop the nuts coarsely.

2 Preheat the oven to 350°F. Oil and lightly flour three 9-inch round cake pans. Sift the flour, baking powder and salt together. Toss half the pecan nuts in 2 tablespoons of the flour mixture. Reserve the remaining nuts for the final decoration.

3 Cream the butter and sugar until pale and fluffy and add the eggs, one at a time, beating well after each addition.

4 Mix the milk with the vanilla extract. Stir the flour into the creamed mixture in three batches, alternating with the milk. Finally fold in the floured nuts.

5 Pour the cake mixture into the prepared pans and bake in the oven for 30 minutes, until the tops are golden brown and the cakes have shrunk from the side of the pans. Cool in the pans for 5 minutes before turning out onto wire racks to cool completely.

6 To make the icing, sift the confectioner's sugar into a bowl, add the egg whites and set the bowl over a pan of boiling water. Whisk for 5–10 minutes until stiffly peaking.

7 Add the vanilla. Remove the bowl from the pan and whisk for 2–3 minutes. Sandwich the cake layers with some icing, sprinkling each layer with some reserved pecan nuts.

8 Ice the top and side of the assembled cake and sprinkle the remaining nuts on top to finish.

INDEX